Sing for your Supper

A DIY Guide
to Playing Music, Writing Songs, and Booking Your Own Gigs

by David Rovics

PM Press PAMPHLET SERIES

PM Press PAMPHLET SERIES No. 0006
SING FOR YOUR SUPPER: A DIY GUIDE TO PLAYING MUSIC, WRITING SONGS,
AND BOOKING YOUR OWN GIGS
By David Rovics
ISBN: 978-1-60486-014-6

PM Press
PO Box 23912
Oakland, CA 94623
www.pmpress.org

Layout and design: Courtney Utt

Printed in Oakland, CA on recycled paper with soy ink.

TABLE OF CONTENTS

INTRODUCTION

I'm often asked for advice on how to do what I'm doing, and I never feel like my answers are very good, mainly because they're far too short and incomplete. I thought I'd make a more serious effort at giving this advice, and that's what you're looking at now.

There's a lot of mythology out there about doing music. Some say it's all about talent, you either have it or you don't. Some say, whether or not you're talented, it's all about luck if you're to make a living at it. I don't think either of those things are true. I think that if you have a deep desire to play music you can get better at it. Once you're good at it, doing it for a living is also possible. But just being good at music doesn't mean you're good at the business end of it, and vice versa. Both are important, and I address both aspects of doing music here.

Obviously there are no guarantees. But I've met a lot of people who want to do music in a more serious way but don't seem to know where to go with it. Often it's because they're not following a good direction in terms of improving their craft. It could be because they don't know how to book a tour, how to get their music out there, or how to manage the business end of doing music. I hope that a careful reading of this pamphlet, and following its advice, will help a wide variety of people wanting to improve various aspects of their craft.

If you're looking to get rich and famous, or to score a major record deal, or to have your videos on MTV or that sort of thing, this is probably not the book for you. This book is not about the music business in that sense. Many musicians out there are writing, playing, and waiting for the record industry to come along and make them famous. Very few of them will be successful. The vast majority—including many who are very good players, singers, and writers—will just be bashing their heads against the wall for the rest of their lives. If that's the path you want to take, I really do wish you luck. You might still find some useful advice in this book, but this is a do-it-yourself guide, how to do these things without the help of big corporations, or even small ones.

A bit more on that…the music industry is part of the overall system of capitalism. For decades it has been eating itself up, just like other industries, to the point where only a few record labels and corporations now control most of the media, including radio stations. It is in their economic interest, apparently, to create a few superstars—and for that matter just a few genres of music—and basically let everyone and everything else rot.

The interests of the people of the world are different, however. People want a wide variety of music to listen to live and in recorded form. While we cannot compete with the music industry in terms of promotion, publicity, and access to commercial media, there is plenty of room in the field for lots of musicians to record CDs, sell thousands of them, tour regionally, nationally, and internationally, and make a decent living at it. The big record companies won't tell you that and they have no interest in helping you do that. For them you're either a star or you're nothing, and there's no middle ground. This book is about exploring the middle ground and being successful at it.

Knowing something about me will be helpful in understanding where I'm coming from and what I can offer you. I'm a singer-songwriter. By music industry standards I'm outrageously "political." That means I write a lot of songs about what's happening in the world. This is part of the thousands-year-old tradition of playing music and writing songs, but it's been largely excised from the "mainstream" (meaning corporate) music scene. People like it, though. They seek it out, and they support artists like me in many ways, because they like the music and they think it's important to spread it around and otherwise support it and the artists who create it. This doesn't mean you have to be a politically-motivated artist to get something out of this pamphlet, but that's where I'm coming from.

For the past decade I've been on tour most of the time. I've done tours in twenty different countries on four continents, and I tour regularly throughout the US, Canada, and six or seven countries in Europe. I have written hundreds of songs, recorded ten CDs, sold thousands of them every year, and have had around a million songs downloaded from the internet. I've had lots of friends, supporters, activists, music fans and occasionally very small independent record labels involved with producing CDs, organizing gigs and helping out in lots of other ways, but by the standards of the music industry it's been an entirely DIY affair. I pretty much book all my own tours, record and pay for all my own CDs with my earnings as a musician, etc.

The guidance I offer in this book is entirely from personal experience. I didn't go and research how other people do things. I'm sure there's lots of advice missing from here, and lots to learn from the experiences of people other than myself. It's by no means a complete guide, but this is what has worked for me.

I strongly believe there is lots of room in the field for lots more people to successfully do what I'm doing, otherwise I wouldn't write this book. On many levels I also think it's an important thing to do.. Culture should be created by and for everybody, not a few pop stars delivering culture to the masses. Also, even without controlling the media, we as artists can have a huge impact. One aspect of what we do is we are part of the media. And just as DIY operations on the internet, community radio, community television, and in print have had a huge impact on the consciousness of people around the world, the same is true of DIY performers and recording artists. Some of us just haven't figured that out yet and are still waiting for the big break that's never gonna come. I hope I can help them change their orientation.

CASTING THE SPELL:
PLAYING, WRITING, AND PERFORMING GREAT SONGS

There are songwriters out there who think that because they're great song-writers they don't need to bother learning how to really play their instrument. There are great musicians who think if they play well they don't need to bother learning to write well. And there are people who think they can write and play well so they don't need to learn how to be good performers. Well, it ain't true. To cast a spell as a singer/songwriter you have to be able to do all three; here are some tips on how you can do it.

PLAYING GREAT SONGS

To get anywhere, you have to play well. There's a common misconception among songwriters—particularly among politically-oriented ones—that content is more important than style: that what you say is more important than how you say it. Although members of an audience or people listening to a CD may not be consciously aware of it (unless they're musicians), the quality of your singing and playing bring a song alive, or deliver it stillborn. Although many other factors matter quite a bit in determining how well a song works, foremost among them is how well you play your instrument and how well you deliver your songs—your style, your musicianship. Here are some tips on improving your playing.

PRACTICE

Becoming a good musician—as with becoming a good songwriter, a good plumber, or a good surgeon—requires lots and lots of practice, like any other form of skilled labor. There isn't necessarily a hard and fast order for these things, but usually you're not going to start writing decent songs until you've become a decent musician.

If you're serious about someday playing music professionally, you have to work at it as a profession for years before you actually start doing any paying gigs. You won't progress if you just dabble around with an instrument now and then. You have to play it regularly, in a focused way, with a set agenda, as close as possible to every day. After a year or two with that kind of focus, you could start getting really good.

IMITATION

In US society in particular, and western societies in general, there is a huge cultural obsession with originality. There are pros and cons to this, but for many artists, especially beginning ones, there are mostly cons. Anyone who's any good at anything probably learned it from someone, or many someones. We're using a spoken language we didn't invent, a musical language we didn't invent, chord progressions we didn't invent, scales, concepts, instruments, etc. If you think you're original, you're kidding yourself, to the detriment of your art. You must imitate. You must steep yourself in the musical traditions that interest you.

Listen to artists that you like, whatever the style of music. Listen to artists that they were inspired by. Listen to them a lot. Learn their songs. Memorize them. Don't just strum the songs, learn to play the songs as closely as possible to the way they played them. Don't worry about being original—eventually people will think you're original; they'll think you have a style of your own, even if you know better...

Generally, the best way to learn songs is to listen and try to play the way you hear it. If, after quite a bit of effort, you can't figure a song out, seek help from live people, other musicians, and/or from books. Especially at the beginning, help from other musicians in the form of formal or informal lessons, along with help from "how to" books such as Mel Bay or whatever, can be invaluable. Songbooks can also help, mainly to have the lyrics so you don't have to transcribe them in order to play, learn and memorize the songs in question. Working out songs or just jamming with other musicians who may be at various levels of ability can also be very instructive. But the key is to listen and imitate.

SCALES AND MELODIES

Every song you do is in a certain key, a certain scale. Learning and practicing scales is not limiting, it's liberating. When you discover that a song is in a certain key, and you internalize this key, you can never play a wrong note. This applies for both "lead" playing or for "rhythm" playing.

One good trick is whenever you learn a song, figure out what key it's in, and figure out how to pick out the melody in that key on your instrument (whatever instrument that is). Then work on playing the song in such a way that you're playing the chords and the melody at the same time. If this concept seems mystifying, an easy way to get a handle on it at first is to learn some basic bluegrass guitar. Learn how to play an alternating bass line. In a song that's in 4/4, typically the bass line is on the 1 and 3, and you strum the chords on the 2 and 4.

Once you master that concept, try playing elements of the melody on the 1 and 3 and strumming the chords on the 2 and 4. Then try expanding that so you're playing more of the melody interspersed with the chords. Once you get good at this, you will impress people (including yourself). This is the basic element of playing an instrument as a solo artist that allows you to really be a solo artist, that takes you beyond just strumming and singing and wishing you had a band. With a solid, steady rhythm, you should learn how to play a song on your instrument while also being able to pick out the melody and play various riffs, especially during instrumental breaks.

Instrumental breaks and riffs are essential to bringing a song to life. Once you're good at this, people listening who aren't particularly musically-inclined will say things like, "it sounds like you're playing two instruments." This is a sign that you're getting the idea, which is not, in fact, a very difficult one—it sounds much fancier than it actually is.

SIMPLICITY, RHYTHM AND TENSION

Especially in light of the above stuff about picking out melodies on your instrument, it's vital to mention that another key to playing well is simplicity. What you don't play is just as important as what you do play. This is especially true if you're playing with other musicians, but also vital for the solo artist.

To play with that steady, rolling rhythm that the good players tend to have, a big factor is not to play on certain beats in a given measure. Which ones you don't play on, as well as which ones you do play on, gives the song it's feeling, whether it's punk rock (all steady downstrokes on the downbeats, with only rare upstrokes), reggae (mostly downstrokes on the 2 and 4), or whatever.

There are good players out there who learned bad technique from the beginning. Often they compensate well enough for it and it doesn't seem to matter, but you might as well avoid that. One thing is to play down on the downbeat and up on the upbeat. Whatever you're trying to do in terms of riffs and melodies and such, you never need to sacrifice this rule. There's always a way to do it without messing up the flow, without playing up on a downbeat or down on an upbeat.

Another vital aspect to playing well is to be relaxed. With music as with many other things, it often seems easier to play a fast or difficult riff if you tense up. In the short term this may be true, or at least seem to be true, but it's never good in the long run. Always stay relaxed, loose. If you're using a pick, it should always be almost falling out of your fingers except at the moment when you're hitting the string(s), when you're gripping it just enough so that it doesn't fall out of your fingers. And when you're fingering the guitar with your left hand, you should just press down hard enough so that the strings don't buzz, never any harder than that.

For singing, to be relaxed is just as important as it is to play an instrument. I could name plenty of great songwriters and instrumentalists who sing with tension in their voice (but I won't). It's quite evident that it adversely affects their singing, tires their voices out much more quickly, leaves them with problems with their vocal chords when they're older, and just doesn't sound as good. People often develop this habit of tension in their throats when they're jumping for a high note that they're not sure they can hit spot on. This is a big mistake. As with playing an instrument, it's always best to be sloppy at first, miss the note, then try again and again until you hit it. Once you hit it that way, you'll always hit it right. Do it with tension and it will sound tense and, generally, you will continue to have problems hitting the note.

OPEN TUNINGS AND VARIETY

Sometimes when I have asked guitarists if they have experimented with open tunings they respond, "No, I haven't mastered standard tuning yet." I have received the same answer when I've inquired about whether they've experimented with other musical instruments. This is as ridiculous as saying, "I haven't tried riding a bicycle yet because I haven't mastered swimming."

Variety is a fundamentally good thing, in music as in life in general. When you experiment with different tunings and different musical instruments and musical styles, it will enrich everything else you're doing musically. Even if you're a relative beginner at an instrument or a tuning, you can always experiment with others. As long as you can manage getting your instrument from one tuning to the other, that means you're ready!

There are books that go into lots more detail about open tunings. (My songbook goes into a bit more detail too, which you can buy or download for free as a PDF file at www.davidrovics.com) Once you've got the basics, though, the best way to learn about them is by trying to play songs by artists that use them, and by experimenting with them. Figure out how to play major, minor, and blues scales in each tuning and you'll learn all kinds of new things. Pick a tuning and figure out how to play a song you already know in that tuning, then try another tuning. Figure out how to pick out the melodies as well as the chords. You'll find that the different tunings lend themselves to different types of moods and songs.

It's the same with different instruments. Without being a master of an open tuning, you can convincingly play a few songs in that tuning if you work them out. By the same token, if you learn a few chords on the mandolin, or spend some time trying to figure out how to use the 5th string of a banjo the way it's supposed to be used, this will inevitably give you new ideas for playing the guitar (or whatever other instruments you play).

INSTRUMENTS AND ACCESSORIES

Far too much fuss is made of what kind of instrument you have. It's also true 99% of the time that the more someone talks about what kind of guitar they have or what kind of electronic toys they use, the more likely it is that they can't play their instrument very well.

Of course you can get a better guitar for $2,000 than you can for $200. But the more you spend, the less the difference in quality. There's a big difference in the under-$1,000 range for sure. After that it becomes much less dramatic. The most important thing is to have an instrument that's easily playable and is made of solid wood, not plywood (if we're talking about acoustic guitars, at least). Plywood guitars are cheap in every sense. They tend to develop problems quickly and otherwise fall apart after a short time.

If you can at least scrounge together a few hundred bucks you can get something that has a solid neck and top, with the rest of the body being plywood, such as a Seagull. Getting closer to the $1,000 range then you're talking about solid wood guitars that improve with age and are made better, though still mass-produced. Well above the $1,000 range you're getting more into hand-made instruments which sound even better, and also tend to be made by smaller companies or individual luthiers.

If you use a pick, the type of pick you use can make a huge difference in how you play and how you sound. A thick pick is great for fast, bluegrass-style picking of individual notes, but is a liability when it comes to rolling, rhythmic strumming (and vice versa). Also, the texture of the pick makes a difference. The smoother-texture picks are easier to use, but lack some of the percussive sound that rougher picks have. I recommend not marrying yourself to one type of pick—always experiment with different picks for different songs and situations. If you're trying to play loudly, say in the street without amplification, you'll want to use a thicker pick. If you're in a more subtle indoor situation, you might want to use a thinner one.

And finally, changing your strings regularly is important. A great guitar with old strings isn't going to sound very good. A cheap guitar with new strings will probably sound better. If you don't like changing your strings every few days, I recommend plastic-coated strings such as Elixirs.

WRITING GREAT SONGS

To succeed as a musician you not only have to be able to play songs well, but also it helps to write songs. The first key to writing good songs is being steeped in the tradition. Know music first. Have it in your blood. Be deeply familiar with at least one musical tradition. Have a couple hundred songs memorized. Be familiar with many more. But there are many other fundamentals to good songwriting, and I will address a few of them here.

MORE PRACTICE

Songwriting, like playing music, is a craft that will tend to improve with practice. Think of yourself as a songwriter. Make time for your songwriting. Live, travel, love, read, do other things that are likely to inspire songs, and then make time for writing the songs and working on them. Test yourself. Come up with things like, "I'm going to write one song per week from something I read in the New York Times," and then do it. They don't have to be your best, most inspired songs. You might throw them out soon after you write them. You might write a good line and not have use of the rest. But doing it often will allow you to get good at it.

TUNING INTO THE MUSE

Part of practicing is finding inspiration and learning how to tune in to the muse. It's out there for everyone, not just "talented" people. You need to be open to it, though, to recognize its importance, and to trust it; trust your subconscious, trust that it knows what's going on. I've always found that if I have an idea for a song it's good to make a note of what that idea is, and then to wait before starting to write the song until I've accomplished two main things. One, I need to have done the research that may be required to write the song well. Two, I need to wait for my subconscious to process the idea of this song. When it's done, which may be hours later or a few days later or sometimes longer, it will tell me. The trick is to be aware of that moment, when there is a certain creative impulse that happens, and to take hold of it without delay.

One of the most important aspects of allowing yourself to tune in to the muse is to prioritize your art above other things. Somehow or other, you need to be able to drop whatever else you're supposed to be doing and write. Sometimes it can be put off, but other times the creative spark will go away and the moment will be lost. It will come back. But there is an element of unpredictability about it that can't just be put off regularly or it becomes stale.

LISTENING AND LEARNING FROM THE WORLD AROUND YOU

You are a participant in the world, of course, but you are also an observer. Like a journalist, you are observing the world around you and writing about your experiences. Or, like a historian, you are reading about or hearing about accounts of events that may have happened long before your time, or, more recently, somewhere you were not; and you're writing about them. Or, more typically in the world of pop music, you're writing about things that require no research, things you've experienced directly, perhaps in a relationship with another individual. In any case, a common theme here is listening— listening to the stories of other people, listening to history, listening to the news or listening to your heart.

You also need to know your subject matter. This may require lots of reading, or lots of experiences with what you're writing. It's easy to read a whole book and only get one short song out of it. But it might be a good one! One trick, though, is to trust someone else who does know their subject material and stick to their details. For example, a well-written newspaper article can be turned into a great song. If I am writing about something basically unfamiliar to me and I allow myself to embellish a line with a detail that I imagine might have been there but don't know for sure, that's often where I go wrong. If you don't know the subject material intimately, you can fake it by sticking to the details that someone else knows intimately. If you're going to make up other details that may make the song have more impact, you need to know your material yourself.

When I say know your material, what does that mean exactly? Obviously, for example, if you're a white middle-class guy from the suburbs (like me), you're unlikely to have much idea of what it's like to be a child in a Palestinian refugee camp, whose parents have just been massacred by fascists. But if you've ever experienced loss in your life, if you've perhaps at least visited a Palestinian refugee camp, if you've read and heard the testimonies of survivors of that massacre, you certainly have something to go on. If you allow yourself to try to write the song, then seek real feedback on it; you may discover that it sucks. You can learn something from this and try again, or perhaps move on to other subjects that are less challenging. There are objective ways of knowing whether you've done a good job or not. If, upon hearing the song, several different Palestinian refugees come up to you at several different shows, crying, telling you how beautiful the song was, you objectively know it's good. If the only people who like the song are other white people from the suburbs, it may not be very good.

I'd say the received wisdom, "write about what you know," is both right and wrong. It's wrong in the sense that just because you may be a white guy from the suburbs doesn't mean that you can't write about things that white guys from the suburbs don't generally experience. It's right, though, in that you must open your heart to be able to identify with "the other" in a profound, emotional way; and you must also do the research that allows you to fill in the gaps, so that you can identify with your subject both emotionally and in terms of shared history and other circumstances—at least enough to create a convincing 3-minute song. Perhaps the most important thing to remember is that we are all human.

THE MECHANICS OF AN EFFECTIVE SONG

Whatever kind of songs you're writing, it's almost always better to put things into the context of a story and to tell a tale rather than deliver a rant. In the most effective songs you are channeling an idea or a feeling, but without imposing your own views and feelings too overtly into the song. The way you tell the story, the words you choose, the meter, the melody, the way you play the song, these things elicit the emotion of the song, not overt proclamations of how you look at things. Always be a Traveler in the Taoist sense: always listening, observing, and turning these observations into songs, bringing other people into the situations you have experienced by telling the story in a way that makes them feel like they were there too—not telling them your conclusions about how the situation felt, but describing it in such a way that they feel it too.

It's also imperative that you be succinct. Usually you don't want more than 3 to 4 verses, and possibly a chorus. Songs are not books, or even essays. Songs are a very restrictive, limited form of writing. Extremely effective when done well, but totally ineffective when done badly. Attention to all kinds of details is vital. Also knowing what you want to say, and saying it, is vital. Beginning songwriters have a tendency to try to write manifestos. I'm not sure if it's possible to write a "good" manifesto in song form. On the occasions where a wordy, informative type of song works, it works because it is sticking to a theme. The manifesto goes from one theme to another, and thus loses it's impact.

Of course, you should give yourself lots of time to allow yourself to make lots of mistakes in the process of writing each song. Treat it with kindness and love; take your time. But be ruthless about it. Never accept a line that doesn't serve an essential purpose. Never accept a rhyme that seems forced. If you're trying to say something that needs to be said but can't find a good rhyme, don't settle for a bad rhyme. Go back to the last line and see what you can change there. Or try the whole part of that verse again with a new tack, because one bad rhyme can ruin a song. You're casting a spell with each song. Each verse, each chorus, each line, each rhyme, all have to hang together. Ask yourself with each verse you write, does this verse really help the listener—on both an emotional and informational level—understand the subject more deeply? Is this verse absolutely necessary to tell the story effectively? Then with each line of each verse ask yourself the same question.

You should also practice writing different kinds of songs. Many songwriters think they're good at one and not another sort of songwriting, and they "specialize." This is a mistake; you will only benefit from experimenting with different styles. Inevitably, perhaps, you'll be better at some types than at others, but you should always keep trying various forms as there are many different ways to effectively illustrate a point. You could even give yourself the exercise of writing a sad song, an angry song, and a satirical song about the same subject.

Another important thing to remember is that the best lyrics will have no impact on your audience if they are not set to the right music; the musical end of the song is just as important for making the song effective or ineffective. Whether you use an A minor chord end or an Am7 chord can make all the difference. Whether there is a slightly longer pause in between the 2nd and 3rd verses of that song can provide a vital space for people to absorb the meaning of a phrase. Experiment with all of these things—use of pauses, types of rhythms, little guitar riffs that can go here or there, length of instrumental sections, cutting or adding a verse, etc.

If all of these elements work together well, the song comes alive and does its magic. If one of them is missing or flawed, the song is dead before it has a chance to live. You have to test out whether all of these elements have indeed come together. You can't possibly write good songs if you can't take feedback as there is such a thing as objectivity in songwriting. This is determined not by the songwriter, but by the audience. Here it is. If a song is sad, it should make people cry. If it doesn't, it's not a sad song. That's objective. If it's funny, people should laugh. If they don't laugh, it's not funny. If it's a rebellious, angry song, it should make people shout. If they don't shout, it sucks.

So you must look for ruthlessness. You must never trust your friends or relatives who say, "That was great." "That was great" is absolutely mean-ingless. Tears mean something. Laughter means something. Words are cheap. If tears or laughter accompany the words, then they may be worth something. Otherwise they are probably the words of someone who is trying to soothe your ego. In our society (I'm talking about the US when I say that, but it's certainly applicable to lots of other societies), most people are loathe to say anything critical. But without criticism, you're unlikely to improve your craft. Don't ask people, "Was it good?" That's called fishing for compliments. Instead, seek out those rare individuals who, when pressed, will at least tentatively offer critical thoughts. When you find these people, treasure them, and seek out their feedback often, no matter how painful it may be.

SOME SPECIFIC TIPS FOR WRITING A GOOD SONG

If you listen to other artists critically, you've probably noticed that it can be very effective to employ certain "tricks." I'll explore a few of them now…

> *Use ALL of the Media*—If you want to have a broader audi-
> ence than progressives who read Z Magazine and listen to
> Pacifica, you need to put yourselves in their shoes. One
> aspect of that is to listen to, watch, and read the media from

which they get their news and outlook. You can, of course, write songs about things that are unfamiliar to most people, but context must be provided. To know the context, you must know what most people are and aren't familiar with. You can also describe the familiar to make a point from those images that the media generally fails to make.

Use the Familiar to Describe the Unfamiliar—Another way you can use the familiar images in the media is to use them to describe the unfamiliar. People can identify with the people dying in the Twin Towers, through a song they can then also identify with people dying in other big buildings that have been bombed by the US Air Force. It's also very useful to use universally familiar things—a mother's love, a child's attraction to flowers, etc.—to bring people into an emotional place where they can viscerally identify with the unfamiliar.

Write Surprise Endings—This is a tool I use a lot, where for most of the song you're describing a familiar scene, or at least familiar enough. Then at the end, the unfamiliar happens, but when it happens, the listener has been emotionally prepared for it and as a result relates to the character in the song in a visceral way. It can take myriad forms. The child loved his parents so much, and then they were killed. The child became a suicide bomber.

"I'm Gonna Write a Robb Johnson song"—Ask yourself how your favorite songwriter would write the song and write it that way. What kind of meter would he use, how would he strum the guitar, how would he phrase things, what kind of internal rhyme schemes would he employ, how much detail would he go into, what kind of riffs would he play on the guitar, would his lines be long or short, would the lengths of lines build or vary, where would the pauses be, etc. You might be surprised at what a freeing exercise this is, and how many good songs might come out of it.

Lose the Chorus—On many occasions Ii've written songs by writing the chorus first and then using the message in the chorus to shape the verses around it. You can then drop the chorus altogether. Whether or not you keep the chorus, it can be a great tool for focusing the verses so you don't drift too far.

Lose the Last Verse—For politically-oriented songwriters especially, there is always the risk of writing that unnecessary last verse that sums it all up. If the song was written well you don't need that verse, and actually you're far better off without it. You don't need to give people the moral of the story, they'll get it just fine.

PERFORMING GREAT SONGS

Say your song is good and say you play it well. You still have to perform it well before an audience, or the spell will not work. There are a lot of factors involved in giving a good performance, here are a few of them. The ones depending on how well you master the mechanical side of the performance are covered in the next chapter.

DELIVERY

You can't be an effective performer if you need to use a music stand or have your lyrics taped to the guitar. It's vital to memorize your material, and have the freedom to look your audience in the eye. You need to be standing up, or depending on the environment, sitting on a stool—not hunched over a small chair. This is both for your lungs and your singing as well as to appear engaged with the audience and with what you're doing.

APPEARANCES

Visuals matter. Part of that is what you look like. Think about how you dress. Whatever your image of your music is, dress accordingly. If being a slob is part of your image, fine. If it's not, then pay attention to what you're wearing. Light-colored shirts and light-colored pants look really bad together on white people. Wash your hair and get it out of your face. Don't tie that sweatshirt around your waist, put it down somewhere off-stage. It's OK to look a bit dapper and professional, everybody will know you don't work for GE. If you have short hair, then keep it short. If you shave, shave. If you have a beard, keep your moustache out of your mouth (unless being a slob is part of your image). Brush your teeth. Do your laundry. Take a shower.

ATMOSPHERE

Noisy bars where people got in for free and aren't there to hear the music are pretty much the hardest places to play. It's remotely possible to harness the energy of an audience like that, but unless you're singing Eagles covers, it's extremely challenging. On the other end of the spectrum would be your folk club that's run for music, with great sound, lights, and an attentive audience that paid to get in and is there to hear you.

Then there are the many places that are somewhere in between. If you take initiative you can often do something to improve the atmosphere; if you don't, it's quite likely that no one else will. Always do a sound check. When you do the sound check make sure someone is checking out the lights too, they often need to be adjusted before the show starts. If there are no stage lights, you can at least try to improvise by having lamps on the stage or having on the lights closer to the stage and keeping the rest of the room dark. It makes a huge difference. This is especially true if you're performing in a lecture hall with fluorescent lights. Turn them off.

BEING ON STAGE

Stages are good, even if it's just a bunch of milk crates with a piece of plywood on top. You should be elevated relative to your audience. You are the performer. This is OK whether you are an anarchist or not. There is an ancient tradition on this planet of performance. Tonight it's you. Tomorrow maybe it will be someone else—perhaps someone else who's sitting in the audience right now. That's fine. You're it tonight; you want to be seen and they want to be able to see you. Don't hide, stand up on a stage. Don't look at the ground, look at your audience.

Your audience wants to get to know you a bit. Be friendly. Don't lecture, don't talk too much, you're a musician, not a school teacher. But talk a bit. Tell a few stories—short ones—in between songs. Random anecdotes are good. Often people may think something you said is funny. Often it will be something you didn't expect they'd find funny. Remember what that was. Say it again sometime.

SET LISTS

Whether you're doing your own songs or the songs of other people, it's vital to vary the songs so you're not doing three sad ballads in a row, or three upbeat hillbilly songs in a row, or three anthemic songs of resistance in a row, etc. How you vary the set should vary depending on the audience.

If you're playing with a band or have a very limited set length, it can of course be useful to have a set planned in advance. But, generally, I recommend more flexibility. You often won't know your audience until you're in front of them—really. At that point you may find that you've included too many funny songs in your set, or too many depressing ones. Then it's good to have songs in mind you can lose and others you can add. Or you may find you're talking too much and the set is too long. Even if you have all the time you want, it's always better to leave the audience wanting more than to play until some of your listeners are getting tired and restless. Give them an intermission or end the show before they get to that point. If they really want more they'll give you encores. If there are no other performers or opening acts on the bill, I think two 45-minute sets is a good, maximum length for a full-length concert. There should always be a good long break in between sets.

ANNOUNCEMENTS

People at professional music clubs are aware of this, but others are not: if people have announcements to make, this should be done at the beginning of a set, not at the end. If announcements are made at the end of a set most won't listen, some won't be able to hear them, though they might like to, and others will be trying to leave the room to avoid the announcements. Some of these may be potential CD-buying customers who will walk past your CD table and leave the room without buying one.

MASTERING THE TECHNICAL SHIT
USING SOUND SYSTEMS AND AMPLIFICATION

Sound systems are not your enemy, they are your friend. If you're playing a house concert or a concert in a small, quiet room, maybe you don't need a sound system, in which case great, don't use one. But if there's an espresso machine, a loud refrigerator, heating or air-conditions sounds, traffic noise, people talking in the back of the room, etc., you're doing yourself and your audience a disservice by not using a sound system.

Sound systems are an instrument unto themselves. You need to learn how to use them, just as you needed to learn how to play your instrument. You need to take time for this by playing at open mikes, playing in the street, practicing through your own sound system at home or at somebody else's place, or however you can manage it.

Once you have the soundsystem set up in a way that sounds good (assuming it's a sound system that's not a piece of shit, and is capable of good sound), then you are working with another instrument that gives you a vastly broader dynamic range to play with, for both your vocals and your instrument. Good mike technique allows you to play quietly and sing quietly, use that whispery voice, sing lower notes than you'd be able to sing if you had to project, sing right into the mike like you're kissing it. You can then get loud for the instrumental sections or whenever, percussively hitting the guitar to make a dramatic interlude much more dramatic, then get really quiet again, quieter than you could get if you weren't amplified. When you sing a loud note you can back off from the mike a couple inches. It will still be loud, but not overwhelming, and this allows you to sing very quietly again right into the mike. Here are some tips for getting the most from your sound system.

MONITORS

It takes practice just to hear yourself through a sound system and not be put off by it. It takes even more practice to use the sound system to your advantage to improve what you're doing, rather than just using it to amplify your music. Whether you're using monitors or not makes a big difference. I'm used to playing without them, but it's very different to hear your music from behind the main speakers than it is for the people in front of them. If you are using monitors, pay attention to how they're set up, because it will tremendously affect your playing. If you have a tendency to bang on your guitar too much, have the guitar pretty loud in the monitors so you will be forced to play more quietly. If you have a tendency not to sing loud enough to hit the notes well, make sure the vocals aren't too loud in the monitors, which will make you sing louder, etc.

FEEDBACK

If a particular note on your instrument is causing feedback, the engineer usually needs to find that frequency on the EQ and lower it. If the engineer is you, the first thing to try is lowering the mid-range frequencies. The best default setting for an EQ is a smiley face. If there is feedback whenever you play anything or say anything, probably the volume is too loud. Never back up from the mike if this happens. Stay close to the mike and have the volume lowered. Backing up from the mike is completely counterproductive and will only make the feedback problem worse, as the engineer may try to compensate by turning you up still louder.

ENGINEERS AND COMPRESSION

Once you get good at using a sound system, the best kind of engineer to deal with is one who sets things up at the beginning and then leaves it alone. If you're not good at using sound systems, then an engineer who is constantly bringing your volume up or down depending on the song can be good, but ideally you want to be good enough not to need that kind of interference. You need to control your own dynamics, and be able to tell the engineer to leave the board alone. Engineers who are used to dealing with amateurs will tend to treat all performers the same way, and you need to be able to (nicely) communicate that you don't need this kind of coddling. If you're good at using a sound system, this kind of treatment can tremendously detract from your performance.

Compression is the enemy of acoustic musicians. Compression is a computerized form of the overly-intrusive engineer. If when you sing or play loudly, the sound cuts out or doesn't get louder when you do, or if you play very quietly but it comes out of the sound system at the same volume as when you're playing loudly, this is a sign that compression is being used. Tell the sound engineer to turn it off. If they get all huffy with you and tell you they're going to turn it down, be friendly but firm with them and explain that you can control your own dynamics and you'd like the compression turned off. If they still don't turn it off, if at all possible consider not using the sound system—or firing nonlethal projectiles at the sound person until he or she comes to his or her senses. Sometimes they're worried that you're going to hurt their speakers if they turn off the compression. Explain to them that you are not a rock band, you are just a person with a guitar, and you're not going to hurt their speakers. Remind them that they are dealing with an acoustic musician, not a band, and everything is going to be OK.

Having said all that, remember that sound engineers are usually not being paid well, if at all; and they're usually trying to do a good job, whether or not they're succeeding. They're also doing a largely thankless job, and they may resent you for doing a job that is generally much more appreciated. Have some respect for them and always thank them at the end of the show, along with the organizers, who are also doing a fairly thankless job. Always remember that whatever is going on, you're the privileged one in this situation and you should be nice to people.

PLUGGING IN AND UNPLUGGING
Always make sure the channel you're plugging your guitar into has been muted before you plug in and before you unplug. Otherwise a very bad noise will happen, and the sound engineer will quite understandably be upset, or you will be, if you're using your own equipment.

USING YOUR OWN EQUIPMENT
There are many advantages to having your own sound system, and learning how to use it. Once you're doing a lot of national or international touring, you probably won't use it that much, but if you're touring locally or regionally by car, it can be very handy as many organizers or venues won't have decent sound systems. You can then also double as an engineer for other events and make some money that way, or use it to wheedle your way onto the bill as a performer. If you're running an open mike or providing sound to events and renting a sound system often, you should certainly consider buying your own system.

> The basics for setting up your own sound system:
> *A mixing board.* A 4-input one is fine for yourself and maybe one other performer, if you're doing sound for bigger ensembles, then you need more inputs. At minimum it should have separate volume and tone controls with at least 3 tone controls per channel (high, middle and low) and at least a 5-band EQ for the whole thing.

Two speakers. You should have one on each side of the stage, elevated on speaker stands to sit slightly above the heads of the audience. Elevating speakers vastly improves their sound and speaker stands are essential, otherwise you need cords to connect these things.

A couple of mikes and mike stands. Boom stands are best—the kind that have a joint that bends in the middle, so you don't hit it with your guitar.

MIKES AND PICKUPS

If you don't want to haul around a whole sound system, certain accessories can be very useful. For sure, one of them is a pickup. If you're really attached to miking your instrument with an instrument mike, fine, good luck. But in most circumstances other than a quiet folk club, it's much easier to have a pickup. If you're using a pickup, get one installed, don't use the ones that you have to wedge into the sound hole. There are lots of good kinds of pickups to choose from. The ones that have microphones in them can be great, but they're finicky. The easiest, most consistent kind is the under-the-bridge Piezo type.

Having your own mike will save you loads of hassles. If you're relying on sound systems at venues and the sound system sucks, you gotta deal with it. But quite frequently a place will have a decent sound system but shitty mikes. You can easily remedy this by traveling with a mike; it's a small thing to carry around and a very worthwhile one.

SUSSING OUT SOUND SYSTEMS AT VENUES

When organizers of a gig tell you there's a sound system, you need to find out what they mean by that. Remember that they might be more used to organizing events for speakers who can make do with whatever 6" speakers are built into the wall or the church or lecture hall. They may even think you can use a lectern. You can't. These things won't do. You need a proper sound system. No matter what they say, 99% of the time the speakers built into the walls of churches and such places are completely inadequate. If they say they had a guy singing through them last week and it was fine, don't believe them. He was probably a tone-deaf member of the congregation and thought the distortion sounded really punk rock. It didn't. It sounded awful.

STREET MUSIC

Playing music on the streets or subways is an art unto itself. Some people manage to make a decent living as street performers, but their art doesn't translate well when they try to take it "indoors." Other people may do very badly at street performance but may become successful touring musicians. I'm more in the latter category, but I did make a living for years as a street musician.

Playing music, doing theater, giving speeches, and other such activities on the street is an ancient tradition. In most of Europe it's tolerated, although that's been changing in recent years in England; and whether or not amplification is tolerated varies from city to city, country to country.

In some places in the US, such as the subway systems in San Francisco, Washington, DC or Atlanta, if you attempt to play music of any sort you will almost immediately be run off by the police. Depending on the city, the mood of the police, your skin color, etc., if you try to play on the sidewalk the same thing may happen , In other cities street music is either tolerated or even encouraged. Cities falling into that category would include New Orleans, Boston, New York City, Portsmouth (New Hampshire), Burlington (Vermont), Seattle, and others.

> It's worth noting that in places where street music is not tolerated, such as the London Underground, the effect of the intolerance by the authorities is not to ban street music, but to drastically lower the quality of it. The best street performers want to perform in places where they will not be hassled by the cops. So when the laws change or whatever, and suddenly all the street performers are being harassed by cops, fined and told to move on, they will go elsewhere to practice their craft. The people who will take their place will be more desperate sorts who are not good players, often have no homes, and are willing to get harassed by the cops because they have no good alternatives.

The Boston area is probably the best part of the US for street music, and it's where I have the most experience playing on the streets. There was a lawsuit in the early 1970's that "legalized" what should already have been legal under the First Amendment but in reality was only "legal" if the local cop was in a good mood or liked you. The lawsuit brought by the Street Artists Guild resulted in clear parameters being set for what was legal and what wasn't. Things like decibel levels measured at a certain distance, how much of the sidewalk you were allowed to be blocking, etc.

WHERE TO PLAY?

The cities or towns where street music works best are always the ones with lots of pedestrian traffic, big open spaces, like very wide sidewalks and parks next to that pedestrian traffic, and not too much car traffic, or ideally no car traffic. This rules out the vast majority of cities and towns in the car-ridden, mall-i-fied and highway-choked United States of America. However, it's a big country and there are still good places left to play.

CITY VS. TOWN, STREET VS. SUBWAY

Other than factors mentioned above, where you play depends a lot on what you do. For example, if you're playing in a busy tourist area like Harvard Square (in Cambridge, Massachusetts), it's a bit sticky. While all the tourists, students, and other visitors are a ripe potential audience, you have lots of competition from other street artists, and the general audience is pretty jaded. They're used to hearing music that's pretty different,and that catches their ear . If you play the guitar with your feet while playing banjo with your hands like my friend Eric Royer does, or if you are a scantily-clad woman singing cabaret in a very seductive way with great microphone technique, or you're an outrageously good, flashy guitarist and you play your instrument upside-down, you may do fine in Harvard Square.

If, however, you're a great songwriter but you don't do covers that people would recognize, or your songs rely more on people listening to get the storyline or hear the words, you may not do well in a place like Harvard Square, but you may do great in the Harvard T stop (the subway) or a similar location. In the subways, wherever they are, the best place for a songwriter type of performer to play is on the platforms.

On the subway platforms people have to wait 5 minutes or, if you're lucky, 10 or 15 minutes for the next train. During that time they can't help but hear what you're doing. Even if it's quiet, non-flashy kind of stuff (like I do, for example), they'll notice what's happening around them after a minute or two, they'll hear a song or maybe two songs, and by then they'll be sucked in and want to give you money and buy a CD. If the trains are running too often it doesn't work. When the trains are running too often, that's when you want to sing your cover songs that everybody will recognize—or learn to play while hanging from your knees, at least if your goal is to make money.

Towns, especially college towns, can be great. The trick is, you can't move in or stay too long. You may be a big hit for a few days in a college town, but then it's time to head on, just like with touring. In big cities, because they have so many visitors and generally so many people, you can get away with playing in the same area frequently, but it's always good to move around anyway.

AMPLIFICATION

In some cities you'll be shut down right away if you use amplification. In others you can get away with it at reasonable volume levels. In some few places, anything goes (I've never been to Barcelona, but that's the rumor).

Whether or not you're allowed to use amplification can make or break a street music situation. If there are cars nearby or other such noises, playing acoustic is really difficult. You risk wearing out your voice by singing too loud too much, and just as importantly, you risk developing really bad habits on your instrument, like banging on it constantly in order to be heard and forgetting how to play with subtlety. On a quiet pedestrian street it can be better to play acoustic, for a variety of reasons, but even there, amplification can be very nice.

There are many options for good amplification systems for street music, much more than when I was doing it. The best thing on the market that I know of is the Crate Limo, a battery-powered amp that sounds great, has all the tone and volume controls you need, inputs for either electric or acoustic guitar and your voice, and a rechargeable battery that lasts a long, long time. If you want, it even has a hole on the bottom to mount it on a speaker stand, but generally for street music purposes that's not necessary. Otherwise, you just need a mike, mike stand and a cord to plug in your instrument and you're ready to go.

For duos or even bigger ensembles, it's still possible to use a Crate Limo by getting a cheap mixing device to split a signal from Radio Shack. Or you can go the route of powering a mixing board and speaker(s) using a deep cycle battery (like a boat battery, similar to a car battery but a bit different) and an inverter. If you get a cheap inverter it'll blow at high volume, but for a solo or other small act that doesn't require a whole lot of power, a relatively inexpensive inverter and boat battery will work fine.

OTHER TIDBITS

Playing street music is a lot like playing in a coffeehouse or bar, but depending on where you set up, you're more likely to be playing for a real cross-section of society, which I often find more interesting than singing for people who already know what to expect.

It's a good general rule of thumb that if you're doing really flashy stuff or singing popular cover songs, you'll tend to do better. But you can definitely suck people in with obscure songs or original music played in a non-flashy way. Doing that is especially a matter of finding the right place to play.

It's also good to try to have good relations with local businesses. More enlightened small or even big business people understand that street musicians are their friends, and bring business. Sometimes they need help understanding this. The Harvard Square Business Association is very pro-street music. They understand that many people visit Harvard Square because of the street music scene.

RECORDING A CD

Getting started in doing music, as with getting started with running any other kind of small business, requires capital to do it right. It requires learning to do lots of new things yourself, but it also requires seeking help from professionals in fields that are not your own in order to do things right. Just because you can play an instrument well, sing well, and write well, by any means doesn't mean you can record well. Recording well requires either learning a lot of skills in addition to singing, playing and writing—or it requires finding people with those skills, and usually, paying them for their time and effort.

The biggest mistake people consistently make when recording their first CD is they think they can do it themselves, or somehow they can do it for free, or close to free. Wrong. You don't have the money, you poor suffering musician you? Tough luck. Go get a fucking job, stop eating out so much, and save some money. Rob a bank. Borrow it from your mom. Whatever. Just stop whining about how expensive it is and deal. Running a small business is expensive. At first, you have to find the money somehow or other, you're not gonna make it from your music (unless you're already successfully playing covers or playing in someone else's band and you're now just trying to branch out into doing your own music).

The other big mistake people make is thinking that it's time to record a CD once they've written one or two good songs. Wrong. Don't record a CD until you have a full CD to record. That is, at least 11 or 12 absolutely stellar songs. 11 or 12 songs where each song makes people weep, laugh, or shout. 11 or 12 songs with great melodies, great lyrics, memorable songs, songs that people have been requesting when you've been singing places, songs that people have been raving about, telling their friends about, marveling at. Songs that people have been asking you, "Is that on a CD?"

FINDING A PRODUCER

If you're an experienced studio musician and you've helped other people make lots of great CDs, you don't need to be reading this section. If you're like most singer-songwriters and you're not an experienced band player or studio musician, then the first thing you need to do is find someone who is. If you live in a city and you've been frequenting open mikes, playing in the streets and playing other gigs, you probably already know more than one person like this. You don't need someone with a long career as a professional producer. You need a really good studio musician whose work you've heard on CDs and liked a lot. If they can record CDs like that, they can probably produce one, and though you may have to pay out something, the cost probably won't be as much as a producer working for some record label. Find someone you like as a person and you admire as a musician, then put your trust in them and work closely together on the details. Give your views on things and let them know how much you value their input, and give them room to implement their ideas.

> The producer is someone who should:
> Have an overview of the project
> Look at how each song is going to be done
> Help decide the best kind of instrumentation
> Work with you to find supporting musicians
> Decide when a song is done and it's time to move to the next
> Figure out what can be done within your budget
> Help find a good, reasonably-priced studio in town

STUDIOS, ENGINEERS, MUSICIANS AND DUPLICATORS

Hopefully your producer will have knowledge about these things and can make some decisions on their own or give you good advice. But basically, if you're doing a CD in a studio with backup musicians, you want people who have studio experience; who are interested in the kind of music you do and, hopefully, in your music in particular; who are good people who are going to listen to your songs before they go into the studio; and will care personally about the results.

Most cities are loaded with music studios, some good and some bad. Listen to CDs by other local artists who have recorded in certain studios and use one of those studios. Don't get sucked in by a studio that supposedly has all the latest equipment. Old equipment can work just fine, it's much more about the skill of the engineer and the quality of the microphones than it is about what kind of software they're using on their computers and whether they have four isolation booths or just two.

There are lots of places to get your CDs duplicated well and cheaply, usually for about $1 per CD if you get 1,000 copies or more.

MULTITRACKING

Multitracking is an amazing thing. Someone can play one part, then someone else can play another with that person, then another, etc., until you have what sounds like a great band playing together or, more often, a big, chaotic mess of lifeless songs that sounded so good live, but...

If you're not an experienced studio musician, don't attempt to multitrack anything. If you're not experienced at playing with a band but you want to have a band playing on your CD, your best bet is either to spend a lot of time playing with a band first and then record the track together with the rhythm section, or get an experienced studio musicians to play your parts. In that case, the producer may opt for the person playing your parts to do it live with the rhythm section, or to multitrack, depending on various factors such as sound quality, schedules, expenses, studio limitations, etc.

MAKING A LIVE CD

One potentially great way around the expenses of doing a CD with a band in a studio -, while still putting out a great CD—is to just record one or more concerts professionally—hiring a professional sound engineer with experience at recording live shows—and then edit it down into a CD. Solo playing is much more forgiving than playing with a band or multitracking, in terms of your rhythm, which may be fine for solo playing but suck for playing with a band (like mine and many others). You could record a CD of just solo material; but if you're going to do that, it seems to me it might as well be done live, so you can capture the feel of a concert, and then most listeners are more open to the idea that you recorded a CD without any instrumentation to make it more interesting than a solo concert might otherwise be.

One of the problems with putting out a live CD is getting good sound quality, because it's harder to record well that way than recording in a studio. Using a venue with good acoustics, a listening audience, minimal background noises such as fans, heaters, espresso machines, and a place with a good sound system and a good sound person are all vital. Then the trick is to go to the studio with the recording and edit out a lot of your talking, which may be fun to listen to once but isn't probably something people want to listen to repeatedly, and edit out some of the applause and whatever else is going on other than the songs themselves. The main thing people want to hear on the CD are the songs, with just enough other stuff thrown in to capture the live feeling.

DEVELOPING A FOLLOWING

To succeed as a musician you have to get started doing tours and playing original music, and to do so you need a following. There are many ways to develop this, and there is no one way that's the best way to do it—the best way is to follow several directions at once, as with so many things. If you follow these different strands I would venture to say that it is a fairly sure route to some kind of success. Of course, even if you are very good at what you do, this success is likely to be limited if you don't have a big record deal, and probably won't result in you getting rich and famous by Hollywood standards.

Also, if you're not really good at what you do, following my advice on finding gigs and promoting your music won't help much. This is because the most fundamental thing about getting anywhere in this business on a DIY level is your dependence on your fans. They are everything. It helps immensely if you have some basic abilities in terms of booking gigs and engaging in limited promotional efforts, but what it really comes down to is your fans, the people who like your music. If people like it, they'll tell their friends. "Viral marketing" is the key—word spreads if the word is good, but it helps to make it easy for that to happen.

PLAYING ANYWHERE AND EVERYWHERE

It's important to know where you're at in your career and to behave accordingly. If nobody knows who you are, a well-publicized gig might only draw ten people. If some people know who you are, the same amount of publicity can bring in ten times as many people. If nobody knows your music yet, you have to admit this to yourself and realize that it's not time to organize a national tour. It's time to keep your day job (unless you prefer to live on the streets and eat out of dumpsters while pursuing your music career—your choice) and play as many free gigs as possible, for the biggest crowds possible.

Go to open mikes. Listen to the other musicians as well; don't be a single-minded stage hog. If there's a protest or a conference or some other event like that happening, offer to sing a couple songs at it. If at first you get lame spots at these events, or get turned down entirely, don't be discouraged.

PLAYING AT RALLIES: REALITY & ETIQUETTE

The standard program for a protest rally goes something like this…First the crowd gathers starting at around 10 am, say, and the program on the stage begins. By noon the march begins. A couple hours later the march returns to the site of the rally or a different site, and there's a second, post-march rally.

You can generally tell which parts of the programs are more valued by the organizers based on the times when they're happening. In a program like the one I've just described, the most important stuff will go on from 11 am to noon, when the crowd will inevitably be biggest. Less important stuff will happen before 11 am, and still less important stuff will happen after the march is done. As experienced organizers know, marches often don't go as planned, and even when they do, many of the people who were there for the initial rally and march often don't show up to the post-march rally.

The best time to play is during the hour or so before the march leaves, that's when there should be lots of music, and maybe some good speakers, too…and to ensure you (or indeed anyone else) are invited to play again, play only for the time-slot they ask you to fill. if they tell you to sing for 10 minutes, play two songs. If at that point they tell you to do another, then do another, but don't play for longer than you're told.

Be a Voice for Music and Culture—For musicians and other people in the cultural field, it's important to understand how valuable what we do is, both in general, and specifically at rallies, conferences, and other such events.

Along with getting media attention, impressing the powers-that-be and educating the public, one of the points of having a rally or other such event is to truly rally the people, to impact the hearts and minds of those in attendance. The power of culture to affect people in this way cannot be overstated. If you talk to people who were at the forefront of the civil rights movement they will tell you that if it wasn't for the music, they might have turned and ran when they saw the riot police and their dogs and water cannon. If you ask people how they got involved with activism of one sort or another, at least half the time it seems their answer will be names like Phil Ochs, Rage Against the Machine, Chumbawamba or a style of music like punk rock. The music is what got them started, and the music is often at the core of what keeps them going.

However, for one reason or another, music is often the last thing to be added to a program, the first thing to be cut, and the element which is given the lowest priority. It's fine to have music playing as a rally is gathering steam or as the marchers are leaving for the march, etc. But that's what canned music is for. If there's going to be live music, then just as with live speakers, there should be a certain respect for the music itself, just as for the speakers. Nobody would ask a speaker to speak while the crowd is gathering or walking away. It would rightly be considered disrespectful. If you are asked to sing at a rally or you are asking organizers to sing at one, you can do your little part not only to advocate for your participation in the event, but to advocate generally for the importance of including culture in the event.

BE AN OPENING ACT
Offer to open for more established musicians if they're playing in your area. If they're playing somewhere you can manage to get to, offer to open for them there. If they tell you to talk to the venue owner or the gig organizer, do that. Accept money if it's offered or just play for free. Union rules don't apply yet—they only kick in (according to my moral compass) after you've got a following.

BE AN ACCOMPANIST
Join a band, if you're able to play an instrument well in that context. Meet people on the road, share your music with them, open for the band here and there if possible with your own material, play at open mikes and other events that you can fit in while you're on tour with the band.

PROMOTING AND REGISTERING YOUR CD
One time when I came out with a CD, I sold a single copy for $12; but if people bought two copies, I'd sell them together for $10 (in other words, $5 each) with the encouragement that people used the second copy to give to a radio programmer or some other person in the music business they may know. This strategy definitely worked at least as well as spending thousands of dollars on advertising.

Make it easy for people with radio shows to get your CD. If they ask for one, send it. If you have a friend who knows somebody at a station, ask your friend to communicate with the radio person they know and send your CD wherever they tell you to send it. If you're sending CDs out cold to radio people you don't personally know, take the shrink wrap off and make it interesting. They're inundated with CDs. You'll be lucky if they even listen to the first 30 seconds of the first track. Your CD should look interesting. I hear even making the packaging you send it in look interesting can make a huge difference.. And those first 30 seconds better be interesting. Whenever possible do live appearances on radio—easiest to manage on community radio. Meet the staff and other programmers when you're there.

Your best promotion for a new CD is doing shows. That's where in all likelihood you'll sell the vast majority of them. You will hopefully develop more and more audience from the web, but many of those people first hear about you because somebody came to a show.

You should always set up your CD table before your show. It should ideally be in a place everybody has to walk past, but where people won't be creating a bottleneck if they stop and look. Make the CD display as wide as possible, so people don't have to reach around each other in order to get at the CDs. People are more likely to buy CDs if there are lots of them on the table. This is called the cornucopia effect, so put out stacks of them. Have a nice-looking email list with a bold header and such, people are much more likely to sign that than a scruffy notebook with "email list" handwritten at the top of the page. Tie a pen to the clipboard with a string so nobody steals it to sign petitions at another table.

If possible, have someone with you at the CD table, so if you get engaged in conversations with people who want to talk to you about your music, or whatever else, there is still someone at the table who can take money for CD purchases. Have a good marker with you to sign CDs; and don't act embarrassed about signing CDs. It's embarrassing enough for many people to ask for a signature, but it's obviously meaningful to them.

As far as royalties go for independent artists getting radio-play, my impression is that BMI is way better than ASCAP. While the media is largely wrapped up in the US, I find there's still a chance for airplay elsewhere in the world. About 90% of my royalties come from the UK. When you come out with a CD, sign up to BMI and register the songs on their fairly user-friendly website. As far as I understand the law (which is not much), the songs are still yours to do whatever you want with them, including registering them Creative Commons, which I also recommend. When you register your songs with BMI you're not selling them, giving them away, or anything like that. You're just allowing airplay of your songs to result in you getting checks for it, that's how the system works.

Although I am a big advocate for providing all of your songs for free download on your website, there are always people searching for songs on iTunes or elsewhere who will not think to look for free ones or who just want to support the arts by paying for them this way. Talking to other professional musicians I know who do not put up all of their MP3's for free, they tend to get somewhat more paid downloads than I do. But this represents a tiny fraction of the number of downloads I get when I make the songs available for free.

The easiest way I've found to make your music available for download is through www.cdbaby.net. They also have lots of useful advice, and they charge a reasonable rate to sell your CDs through them as well. Also, once you have a CD on their site for sale, it's just a matter of perusing their website and clicking a few things to get all of your music up for sale through iTunes, SnoCap and other services. Much easier than registering yourself through these services, and CDBaby charges next to nothing for this convenience.

BUILDING A PRESENCE ON THE WEB

Playing your music live is one of the best ways to get that vital following, but you need to make it easy for the word to spread. You have to have an easy-to-find website, like www.davidrovics.com. If people can spell your name they can find your website. You have to maintain and grow your email list. You have to have a page on MySpace, lots of free, full-length MP3's for download, and videos of you singing live for folks to find on YouTube.

Buzz has always been where it's at. You want people talking about you. A major record deal and millions of dollars can create buzz on just about anything, but even then, it has to be good for it to keep going long-term. With all the power of the internet you may never match the kind of buzz that conventional publicity can generate when they spend enough money on it, but you can certainly do far more for free than could ever have been imagined by record executives a couple of decades ago.

The Argument for Free Downloads

Sales are down massively for the major labels. The age of the internet is democratizing the airwaves to a significant degree. The major labels, while still making lots of money and still having almost exclusive access to the major media, still feel threatened. They have retaliated with a sustained propaganda blitz aimed at convincing people in the US and around the world that downloading music for free is essentially a criminal activity.

Still, my impression is that overall the internet—and the free sharing of culture that has so far been inherent to the internet—has been overwhelmingly positive for most artists. For most professional, independent artists who are locked out of "conventional" media and publicity, overall the internet has been a very positive development. I would also suggest that the artists who have made lots of material easily available for free download have benefited more than those who have not. This is one of today's key issues for all musicians, so I have devoted much more time to it in an essay at the end of the pamphlet.

YOUR WEBSITE

If you're a Luddite, stop being one. You're a songwriter and you're running a small business. These are contradictory things in terms of left- and right-brain activities, but they're both crafts that can be learned well, or at least well enough. You need to be able to run your business. Consider learning a bit of HTML a top priority, a lot of helpful books and websites exist.

If nobody of professional quality volunteers to make a website for you for free and graphic design is not your area of expertise, you should hire someone. You are the one, however, who should be updating it. By learning a few commands it's easy to keep a website updated in many day-to-day ways—updating your gigs page, and even uploading MP3's, pictures, and all kinds of other stuff.

Your website should provide all of the information that your fans could want in a way that's easily accessible through links on your main page. The people going to your website are generally going to be looking for the following:

> *Upcoming Gigs*—Fans will want to know where you are playing and when, and who else is on the bill. This should also include information on how they can book a gig in their area.

Press Materials—This includes all the materials that media or gig organizers might need. One of the most useful things will be a good quote from a media outlet or luminary, you should seek these quotes out and put them at the top in the press section and perhaps on the main page of your website. The other things you should include are:

Your Bio—Display a short bio that explains who you are and what you're doing

Links—Place links to CDs and concert reviews

Photos—Have available high-resolution photos of yourself with the name of the photographer available for download

Posters—Create and post your posters that people can download as PDF files with blank space at the bottom for filling in details about the local show

Contact Information and Email List—This will allow people to get onto your mailing list and collect information about the city, state and country where they live.

Music Information where to find your lyrics, additional information on your songs, or where they can buy your albums

Free Music—This will probably be the biggest reason people visit your website—and why they will spread the word about it. Don't put up clips of songs, put up songs in their entirety. Don't just put up a few, if you put up all of them people will be much more impressed, the buzz will be bigger, and better things will tend to happen. Whether you will end up losing CD sales as a result is not at all a certain assumption. Whether you will gain more of an audience around the world is certain.

There are many websites where you can host unlimited numbers of songs for free, no matter how many songs are downloaded. I use www. soundclick.com. If people record your shows or videotape them, you can encourage them to put stuff up on the web. They can put up entire concerts in MP3 form at www.archive.org, or put up videos they've shot of individual songs on YouTube. On your free music page you can put in links that take people directly to your section of these websites.

Your Online Store and Paid Downloads—There will always be some fans who want to buy your music and support you, so have a link to your online store, whether that's run by CDBaby, yourself, or another service.

Links to Social Network Sites—Set up a MySpace page and link to it from your main website (and vice versa of course). Other sites are YouTube, Facebook and Flickr, people are looking on these sites for you who may not look elsewhere. You'll get lots more downloads from a video if you put it up on YouTube than if you just host it directly from your site, and a lot of young people hardly ever leave MySpace when they're on a computer.

ORGANIZING A TOUR

OK, so you've got a great repertoire of songs, perhaps a combination of obscure covers and originals, or maybe just originals. You've got a great-sounding, good-looking CD full of great songs. You've got a spiffy website with all kinds of free music and useful info on it. You've spent years living in different cities, playing with different musicians, singing at open mikes, doing the occasional gig here or there. Or maybe you've been doing that in one region, but all the while meeting more people from different places, playing with different musicians, accumulating contacts. Maybe you've got enough contacts to do one regional tour; maybe enough to do a bigger tour. But you're gonna try to organize one, in any case.

It's a difficult time when you first start touring. It's easiest if you wait until the time is really ripe. Just as you waited until you had an entire CD's worth of good songs before you put out a CD, you're best off waiting to organize your first real tour until there are certain conditions.

Hopefully by now your music should have created at least a bit of a buzz on the internet. You're getting more friends on MySpace, you're getting occasional emails from people you don't know but who have heard your music somewhere and like it. They're wondering if you're going to be playing in their area. Maybe they're offering to organize a show. You should have had success building a following locally. People are coming to your shows and they're encouraging you to take your show on the road. From traveling, touring in a band or as an opener, or moving around, you should have at least some contacts in different places, at least a few dozen folks on your email list in states or countries you want to play in.

With this minimal scenario in place, you might be ready to try to do a tour, but you can be sure it won't break even. If I want to tour in a new region or a new country, I either wait until I have some great institutional gig that pays expenses and all that, or I just figure that the first tour of a new area will not make money. Not making money of course means you're actually losing money, since you presumably have to pay for rent and other expenses back home. It's tough. Savings are good. Most small businesses fold in the first year because they are undercapitalized. Credit cards can be useful, but obviously a mixed blessing.

The other big factor, of course, is whatever day job you may be doing at home. It's usually difficult to find jobs that allow you to travel and tour whenever you want to, but if you quit your day job before your first real tour, that could be a very bad idea. Once you're making a reliable living as an artist, of course, it tends to get progressively easier. Until the time that that happens, if it does, life will tend to be challenging.

GETTING STARTED

You should start planning your tour months in advance of doing it. Plan on where you're going to go, based on where you think you have contacts with fans, other musicians, people who run venues, etc., so you can get some gigs in that area. See if you can get commitments from people in certain places to organize something for a certain date. Use a map. Let's say you've got three good contacts in different parts of the midwest who have offered to organize gigs for you in their towns. Say these towns are Toledo, Chicago and Minneapolis. You could start in Toledo on the weekend, plan on playing in Chicago mid-week, and Minneapolis on the following weekend.

Then the trick is to fill in the dates in between.

Depending on factors like time, money, and ambition, you could be conservative and plan a week-long tour (though that would not allow time for a round-trip), or try booking something longer. This decision can also depend on where you're coming from and how you're getting back. Generally, touring in the US requires a car. Although it's conceivable to organize a tour using buses and trains, mass transit in most of the country is abysmal and a huge hassle.

If you're driving your own car to do this tour, then you'll be needing to take your car home again, so you'll need to book a tour that goes out and back. If you're flying and renting a car, it's almost always much cheaper these days to return the car to the airport where you got it, so unless you have some great gigs or tight timing or both, it usually makes the most sense to book the tour in such a way that it goes in a loop bringing you back to your start.

USING YOUR WEBSITE

Once you have a basic tour plan in mind, put it up somewhere prominent on your website—certainly in your "gigs" section, but perhaps on the main page and elsewhere. Announce to your friends on MySpace that you're planning this tour. Let visitors to your website know that you're looking for other dates in the area. Encourage them to email you if they have any ideas, and to see if their friends have any ideas. Make sure they know that you don't have a booking agent or any of that stuff, that it's a DIY affair, and it won't be successful without their help.

USING YOUR EMAIL LIST

Your email list should be divided by state. You should be conservative in how often you bother your entire list or even regional parts of it. Send out too many emails and folks will quickly start ignoring them and unsubscribing from your list. Once a month is a good rule of thumb.

You can email your entire list and ask them if anybody knows someone in Ohio, Illinois, or elsewhere in the region you're going to. It's good to have other things to tell your entire list, not just to email the whole list for something like that. Better if you're announcing some new songs that are now online or something else of general interest to folks on your list.

You're likely to have more luck emailing folks targeted regionally. People in Toledo will be more likely to know folks in Ohio and Michigan than folks in Connecticut will. They're also more likely to pay attention to an email where the subject line mentions their state. Of course, they're even more likely to pay attention to an email addressed to them specifically as individuals; but if you're doing that, I'd suggest making each email personal, not just with their name on top and the same email following each one. People can tell. And it's time consuming.

If someone responds positively to an email about organizing a show in their area, make sure to save their email in a folder marked "booking," or something like that. In the future, these contacts may be more useful than many others. Or they may fall off the face of the earth, but it's worth saving them and bothering these specific individuals next time you're coming.

COMMUNICATING WITH ORGANIZERS

Always respond to phone calls within 24 hours at the most. Always respond to emails within 48 hours. If you're not going to be able to do these things for some period of time, tell in advance the people you're working with. If you can't deal with these simple rules of conduct in communicating with people you're working with, you will probably develop a reputation as someone who is not reliable. By the same token, if you commit to a plan, commit to touring in a certain area, or commit to a gig—especially the latter—don't change your plans. If you do, people won't want to work with you in the future—for good reason.

Always bear in mind that the people you're working with are probably doing whatever they're doing, be it a little or a lot, out of the goodness of their heart. They believe in the importance of music, or political music, or you, or all of these things, and they're organizing something because they want to do something useful, and because they want to help you. When you're asking things of them, it's always important to remember this. It's OK that you need certain things if you're doing a gig, and if they've committed to organizing something then hopefully you can count on them and you don't need to walk on eggshells. At the same time, remember that they are doing you a favor. Hopefully they get some benefits from it, too; but if any of those benefits involve money, you can bet that they're not earning much at it.

It's good to know what you can expect, in general and specifically, from certain organizers. This depends on where you're at in your career, whether you're visiting a place for the first time or not, and on the experience level of the organizers. But whether you're playing for tips, or for a cover with no guarantee, or for a guarantee from a well-funded student organization, there are certain things you want to happen for each gig.

Some of these things may not be realistic, depending on the various circumstances; but there are certain things you want to at least talk about with organizers of gigs where you're going.

PROMOTING THE SHOW

Inexperienced organizers may not realize that they are the ones who primarily need to promote the show. From afar, it's very unlikely that your email list is going to draw much of an audience by itself. And from afar, that's about all you can realistically do from your end. The rest is up to the organizer of the gig, and it's up to you to cooperate with them to make their job as easy as possible.

If you're doing a gig where there's a financial guarantee or if you're working with an organizer who's clearly had lots of successful experience at putting on concerts, then you probably can relax. But if you're working with someone who may not have much experience (including most student groups who may be paying you a guarantee but may not have the first clue about how to promote a show), it's useful to give them tips on how to organize a show.

Many touring musicians have never done it themselves. You should give it a try. It's hard, tedious work. Some people enjoy it. Most do it because they feel like there's value in it and they're trying to be useful to their community.

The trick is creating a buzz. Any one form of publicity by itself is probably inadequate. People need to hear about a gig from various sources before they're likely to go. It also helps immensely if they've heard of you before. Hopefully the organizer will do some or all of the following to promote your show:

Try to get the local community radio station on board to promote the show with a PSA or cart. Try to get you live or phone interviews with radio programmers, and make sure (with your help) that all the local programmers who want your CD have it. Get your show listed in the community radio station's events calendar.

Get your show listed in the music calendars of all the local daily and weekly newspapers. Ask people at the papers who cover the arts if they might do a preview and/or review of your concert.

Put up nice-looking posters in key places around town weeks ahead of the show, and make the rounds to ensure those posters stay up.

Call all of their friends and tell them about the show. They should encourage their friends to do the same. Word of mouth is absolutely vital.

Send out at least two announcements—one a week or two in advance, and another a couple days before the show –to relevant local email lists, such as any related to local cultural events or local activist events.

Go to other events that might draw a similar audience to yours, and hand out flyers about your concert.

Bill your concert, if at all possible, as a bigger event. Even if the concert is not a benefit, it can still be sponsored by an activist organization. Add an opening act and a sponsoring group and it can be billed as a "peace concert," or a "festival for global justice," or "celebration of resistance," or whatever seems appropriate.

Encourage the venue to do their own publicity and to advertise your show on their website and email list. Post your concert on local websites that people visit to find out what's going on around town, in addition to the email lists, print publications, etc.

My friend Ben Manski in Madison, Wisconsin is a very experienced organizer of events of all sorts. The way I remember him describing how to tell whether the efforts of the organizers have coalesced to create an authentic buzz, is by the time the event is close to happening you should be hearing about the event from various people who don't know you're the one organizing the thing.

PICKING VENUES

Just about any place can be turned into a decent concert venue with effort, but you can encourage organizers of your gigs to try to get venues that are conducive to live music. These are usually places that people know, that regularly have live music and with a reputation for putting on quality musical acts, and that are easy to get to. Ideal venues are places that charge a cover, otherwise it's going to be difficult for you to make any money, unless your show has institutional sponsorship of some kind. If you're playing for tips, that can make a lot of sense when you're just starting out, or you're playing in a town you've never played in before; but generally it's a good thing to move on as soon as possible. Audiences will listen and respect what's going on in a venue that charges a cover, and you'll be more likely to get paid—a win-win situation. You can always insist that no one be turned away for lack of funds, so your crust punk buddies can still come to the show.

Unless you're catering to religious Muslims or certain other people, it's generally preferable to play in places that serve beer and food. People usually like that. You can still draw a great crowd to a Unitarian church gig, but most people prefer to be able to have refreshments other than juice and cookies when they go to a concert. On the other hand, it's also great to play gigs where Muslims feel comfortable, and where people under 21 can come, too. So good luck trying to juggle that one.

HOUSE CONCERTS

It's always good to suggest to people that you can do house concerts. In the folk scene in certain regions of the country and world, house concerts are commonplace. In other places they're unheard of, but shouldn't be! They will often have fewer people at them, but the people who come will tend to be particularly dedicated music fans, especially if it's an established house concert series. The standard is a pot luck dinner followed by a concert, usually in someone's (large) living room, with no amplification. Usually the people hosting the concert take care of asking for donations from people. To get around the legal issues involved with charging a cover in a noncommercial venue, the standard thing is to ask for a "suggested donation" of $10 or such. When you and local organizers advertise this concert, you should only have the email and phone number of the hosts on the website as most people don't like their street addresses appearing so publicly. Fans can then call for the address.

LODGING

Some organizers will assume you need a hotel room or a nice guest room in somebody's house. Many will assume you have lodging worked out. Others will assume you're happy to crash on some stinking couch in the hallway by the kitty litter.

Teenage anarchist punks will criticize you for being bourgeois (or at least they do that to me), but most people will go crazy if they don't have a nice place to sleep most nights. Many people who have tried to make it as touring musicians but who have failed ask me how I do it, because the touring lifestyle drove them nuts. I answer: having my own room to sleep in every night.

This is surprisingly easy to line up, if you just ask. If you explain to people you need to have your own bed in your own room to sleep in, 90% of the time that's all the explanation that is needed, and they will understand what this means. Even if they and all their friends are poor and none of them have a proper guest room, there is usually someone with an office in their house with a futon in it.

It's really important to learn to make yourself at home in other people's homes. Don't walk on eggshells, it's not sustainable. Be polite and sociable, of course. If you don't like people and you don't like being sociable with them on a daily basis, the life of the touring musician is not for you. Whether or not you are a nice person makes all the difference in terms of whether people want to organize stuff for you in the future. However, for your own sanity, you also need to be able to relax completely in somebody else's home. Most people who are used to hosting traveling musicians will be at ease with this, and most others will not be too mortally offended by you grabbing a towel from their closet and using their shower without asking first.

Traveling in a camper van or some other such vehicle can also be really nice, and a good way of being civil while avoiding too much socializing, if that's a lot better for you. There are, of course, the problems of weather, seasons, and the price of gas to contend with in that case; and if you're doing a very busy tour, it may or may not be any cheaper than paying for a cheap hotel room every night.

FLYING WITH AN INSTRUMENT
Some people travel with heavy flight cases so they don't have to worry about getting on a plane with a guitar. I deal with repetitive strain injury in my wrists from my career as a typist many years ago, so for me this is not an option. If you want to avoid developing RTS, tendonitis, or other physical problems, you're also probably best off leaving the flight case for special occasions and otherwise just travel with a gig bag (soft case).

The vast majority of time you can bring your guitar on the plane if it's in a gig bag. Usually you can even bring it on if it's in a hard case or a flight case, too (but your arm might fall off by the time you've carried the guitar to the gate). There are exceptions, so let me explain how it generally works…

If you're flying on a small plane, you'll need to gate check the guitar. I have had a guitar damaged from gate-checking it. Someone apparently dropped it hard on the way from the plane to the baggage cart. But this could potentially happen with a flight case that you check with your luggage, too. It's best if you can bring the guitar on with you, but generally I find gate-checking works out fine. If it's in a gig bag I think they're more likely to be gentle with it because it's so obviously fragile, so I'd suggest either use a gig bag or, if you must, a flight case, but not anything in between, like a typical hard case.

There are some airlines like Delta and America West who would make you gate check your guitar regardless of the size of the plane. A Musicians' Union boycott changed Delta's mind. Although this is no longer true for either, it's worth checking the rules with the airline before you fly.

TRAVELING WITH OTHER STUFF

As a solo musician you can generally get away with doing domestic tours without having to take your own vehicle (unless you want to for other reasons), and without having to mail anything ahead or pay extra for extra baggage (unless you're doing an extremely long tour).

Wheeled suitcases are a must. Get two of them, and make sure one of them is equipped with a strap setup for wheeling a second suitcase behind it. In one suitcase you'll have your clothes and other odds and ends. In the second suitcase you'll have your CDs and other merchandise. When you're going from the rental car to the airport or vice versa, or if you're traveling by some other means, with two wheeled suitcases in one hand, guitar over one shoulder and perhaps your bag with your laptop and stuff in it over the other shoulder, you're all set, and you even have one hand free for opening doors and such. It's a very sustainable way to go.

MORE ON FLYING AND RENTING CARS

There are lots of very competent travel agents you could use, but I have found that doing it myself is actually easier. Here are some tips on being your own travel agent using websites like Expedia or Orbitz:

Research your flights. Look at standard round trip, multi-city tickets that begin and end in different places, and one-way tickets; now you can find these tickets cheaply.

Book in advance, if possible well over a month ahead. The prices often rise dramatically if you wait until there's less than two weeks before your flight.

If you can, check flights on different days or at different times. The price of the ticket can vary a lot, though you should balance sleep and quick flights with your budget.

Get a credit card with frequent flyer miles—and keep track of them. You'll need one to get a rental car anyway.

Research rental car costs. The cost of rental cars varies wildly depending on the airport, and then also depending on whether you're returning the car to the same airport or a different one.

Don't get the insurance on your rental car. If you're renting the car with a credit card, for example VISA, the card comes with insurance for cars you rent. Check yours out.

Get a GPS. For the traveler, it's really silly not to have one. You can't possibly carry about enough maps to get you to all the places you're going.

TIPS ON TOURING INTERNATIONALLY

Touring in other countries is a lot like touring in the US, but with some differences.

FINDING THE GIGS

In the age of the internet, the world is more connected than ever. If you have lots of free MP3's on the web and a strong presence there, word will tend to spread. These days more than ever, folks in other countries will stumble across your music online somehow or other. You can of course also be more proactive about it, send CD's to relevant radio programmers, travel around in countries you want to tour in and make various connections with local social centers, infoshops, pubs, cafes, open mikes, sidewalks, festivals, and wherever else music might be happening.

But these days if you're getting offers for gigs in different parts of the US, you're likely also getting them from countries in Europe and elsewhere. Maybe you're thinking someday you'll tour there and haven't done it yet. If so, I'd encourage you to venture out there at some point, and realize that just as it started slow and then after a while took off more at home, it'll probably follow the same trajectory elsewhere.

BOOKING AND TRAVEL LOGISTICS

You can book a tour in Europe, for example, just as you would book a tour in the US, with some differences. One is language. In countries where real fluency in English is more limited, I've found that if you don't speak the language, it works far better if you find someone willing to basically organize the tour for you, and to communicate with everybody in their own language.

Another logistical issue is distances and travel. Outside of certain cities in the US, you know that parking will be easy, driving will be the most practical way to get most places you're going, and if a place is 150 miles away you can probably drive 65 mph down the highway and get there in a little more than two hours. In other places this does not always hold true. If driving, leave yourself loads of time to get wherever you're going; and make sure you figure out in advance how you're going to be able to park overnight wherever you're staying. And in your cost planning, make sure you factor in the cost of tolls, not just the cost of the rental and gas.

MAILING AHEAD
One way to deal with the train vs. car issue is to travel by train, but mail boxes of CD's ahead in advance to the various places you'll be going. Of course this requires estimating how many CD's you might sell, but you can figure these logistics out and do it. Then you can travel with only one suitcase instead of two (plus your instrument of course).

CUSTOMS AND IMMIGRATION
It's a good idea to mail your product ahead of your tour. It's less likely to raise suspicion. This is also one benefit of traveling with a flight case—this usually means that when entering passing through immigration (if not customs) you don't have an instrument hanging from your shoulder. If you're going the route of getting proper work permits and all that, that's great. I've tended to skate around that, which is probably not wise. I was recently banned from entering Canada for one year, because I said I was going to visit friends, but was actually going to play a gig. This was a bad idea on my part (and a fairly draconian reaction on the part of Canadian authorities, if you ask me). It's best to tell the truth, at least to say you're going to do some performing, but it's all minor stuff and you're barely covering your expenses (which is likely to be true anyway!). And if you don't have CD's with you, or much other stuff, you look better. It's always best to look presentable, take out your piercings, take a bath, wear normal-looking clothes, etc.

LANGUAGE
In Scandinavia or Holland, or certain other places, you can behave as

normal in terms of language—nearly everyone speaks English. In most countries, though, English fluency varies a lot. For best results—and in many countries to have any results at all—you need to do something about this. My favorite solution is to have someone interpret for me on the stage, to translate the random stuff I say before I sing a song; just remember to say less because translation causes everything to take twice as long. The other part of the solution is to travel with, or arrange use of, an LCD projector at all gigs in certain countries—this so you can project onto a screen lyrics that have been translated. You can also hand out translations of lyrics but it's much more effective to project them. If someone's gone through the trouble of doing translations of enough of your songs, lining up use of LCD projectors is a relatively small hurdle.

COMMUNICATION

Free wireless signals are easier to find in the US than in most other countries, but they're pretty much everywhere if you know where to look. In terms of phones, for calling internationally (including within Europe, but outside of the country you're in), use a phone card that you can buy at many (but not all) convenience stores. For calls within a country you can get a cheap phone that you can use anytime you're anywhere other than North America, Mexico and certain other countries that uses the CDMA system. In Europe, the economical way to go is to have a different SIM card for each country. Thus you have a phone number people can call you on in each country and where you can generally receive calls for free. When you go to a new country you just replace the SIM card; you'll have a different phone number, but otherwise your phone is ready to use just like before. The standard, inexpensive way to go for travelers is "pay as you go," where you get a Top-Up Voucher at most any convenience store to put more minutes on your phone.

FINAL WORDS

If there were three very simple messages I could communicate to anyone interested in making a living as a singer-songwriter, or as a musician generally, it would be in the form of three "don'ts" and three "do's": You don't need to go to music school to be a good musician; you don't need to get recognition from record labels or commercial radio stations to be a good songwriter or creative artist; and you don't need to "get a job" in order to make a living as a performing artist.

You do need to steep yourself in the tradition; to practice your craft obsessively (or at least diligently); and to answer your emails promptly.

I hope to see you on the road and in the streets! If anybody has any comments they might be willing to share about this DIY Guide, I'd love to hear from you—just go to www.davidrovics.com and drop me a line...

THE RECORDING INDUSTRY ASSOCIATION OF AMERICA VS. THE WORLD

The Recording Industry Association of America (RIAA), representing massive multinational corporations with tentacles in every corner of the global economy including the music business, has just won a lawsuit against a mother of two who refused to be pushed around. Jamie Thomas' pockets were not nearly deep enough to mount the kind of legal defense for the occasion, but she rightly thought that paying an out-of-court settlement of several thousand dollars for the "crime" of sharing music online was ridiculous. So she told the RIAA they'd have to take her to court. They did, and they won.

The fact that one of these cases actually went to trial, the amount of money involved, and the fact that the defendant could have been your neighbor, a middle-aged single mother of two who was not selling anything, but was just engaging in commonplace song-swapping via Kazaa's peer-to-peer network, has made this case newsworthy. But what lies beneath it are the ever-growing tens of thousands of people who have been spied upon, harassed and threatened with lawsuits if they didn't pay the RIAA thousands of dollars for sharing copyrighted music in a way the RIAA, the US government, the World Trade Organization, etc., deem inappropriate.

In spite of the RIAA's campaign to staunch the profit losses of it's corporate members by waging a campaign of fear and intimidation against your average everyday music fan, the numbers of legal and "illegal" downloads continue to rise rapidly. However, the industry's campaign is not just about robbing working-class, American music fans of hundreds of millions of their hard-earned dollars. The music industry is waging a war for the hearts and minds of the people of the US and the world, spending tremendous amounts of money on advertising campaigns to convince us of the rightness of their cause and the wrongness of our actions.

The RIAA is both powerful and desperate. They are a multibillion-dollar industry that has been "suffering" financially for years, and they are up against the very nature of the internet—or peer-to-peer sharing of information in whatever form (stories, songs, videos, etc.). The internet has given rise to unprecedented levels of global cultural cross-pollination, and it has led to a democratization of where our news, information, music, etc., comes from that has not been seen since the days of the wandering troubadours who went from town to town spreading the news of the day.

The RIAA is trying to use a combination of the law, financial largesse, and encryption, along with other technologies, to try to reassert their dominance over global culture. But perhaps most importantly, they are trying to reassert the moral virtue of their positions—the rightness of their positions vis-à-vis the concept of intellectual property and the notion that the fear campaign they're engaged in somehow benefits society overall and artists in particular.

The success of their campaign to convince us that the average person is essentially part of a massive band of thieves can be easily seen. Look at the comments section following an article about the recent lawsuit, for example, and you will find people saying they thought Ms. Thomas was wrong, but that the amount of money involved with the lawsuit isoutrageous. You will find people admitting that they also download music illegally, and they feel bad about it; but it's just too easy to do, is there, and the music in the stores is too expensive.

Obviously the idea of anyone being financially bankrupted for the rest of their lives because they shared some songs online is preposterous, and very few people fail to see that. But the idea that Ms. Thomas did something wrong is prevalent, even among her fellow "thieves," and I think it needs to be challenged on various fronts.

"WE'RE DOING THIS FOR ARTISTS"

The RIAA represents artists about as effectively as the big pharmaceutical companies represent sick people. I'll explain. The vast majority of innovation in medicine comes from university campuses. The usual pattern is Big Pharma then comes in and uses the research that's already been done, then to patent it, and finally turn it into an obscenely profitable drug (especially if it's good for treating a disease common among people in rich countries). They then say anybody else who makes cheap or free versions of the drug is stealing, and by doing so we're stifling innovation and acting immorally.

Similarly, the vast majority of musical innovation happens on the streets by people who are not being paid by anyone. The machine that is the music industry then snatches a bit of that popular culture, sanitizes it, and then sells it back to us at a premium. They create a superstar or two out of cultural traditions of their choosing, and to hell with the rest of us. Sometimes the musicians they promote are really good, but that's not the point. The point is that if the RIAA were truly interested in promoting good artists, they'd be doing lots of smaller record contracts with a wide variety of artists representing a broad cross-section of musical traditions. But as it is, if it were up to the RIAA we'd be listening to the music of a small handful of multimillionaire pop stars and the other 99.9% of musicians would starve.

The overwhelming majority of great music in the US (and most certainly in the rest of the world) is not supported by the RIAA. Rather, it is marginalized as much as possible. "Payola" is alive and well. The commercial radio stations are paid to play RIAA artists, and paid not to play anyone else. A strategic, financial decision is made to promote a few styles of formulaic anti-music, each style represented by a few antiseptic pop stars—the lowest common denominator that can be created by the corporations behind the curtain. On the other hand, the overwhelming majority of great writers, recording artists and performers is ignored, denied record contracts, promotion, airplay, distribution, etc.

In short, the RIAA does their best to stifle art, at the expense of money. They represent some artists, no doubt—a few very well-off ones, the few (occasionally very talented) beneficiaries of their money-making schemes. In the US, even the system through which royalties are distributed ends up benefiting only the industry and a few pop stars. The comparatively little airplay independent artists receive is measured by organizations like ASCAP in such a way that it is largely ignored, and royalties we should be receiving end up in the pockets of the industry.

"DOWNLOADS HURT CD SALES OF OUR ARTISTS"

OK, so the RIAA's claims to represent artists in general may be laughable, but surely they have a point when they complain about the annually decreasing CD sales of Coldplay and the Rolling Stones? Even if they are just a cartel representing the interests of the few and trying to prevent access or representation by the many, surely suing average music listeners is at least some kind of response to their artists losing sales to these free downloads?

The kind of logic that sees loss of CD sales for major label artists as a direct response to being able to download their music online for free is flawed. It assumes that people would be buying the CD's of these artists were it not available for free. The reality, I suggest, is very different, and also hard to measure with any degree of accuracy.

With the rise of the worldwide web has come an explosion of interest in an ever-broadening array of music. People from all over are downloading for free *and* paying for new music. When big-time artists get loads of conventional publicity, and everybody can't avoid knowing that Janet Jackson has a new CD out because this news is covering the sides of every bus in the city, many people will go ahead and download tracks from her new CD if they can find them on the web for free. But would they bother buying the CD in the current, rich musical environment of the internet otherwise? Or would they just move on and download other stuff from the independent artists they're constantly discovering out there on the web instead?

I'd suggest the latter, and I'd further suggest that there is no reliable way of knowing whether or not I'm correct. If the major artists are losing sales because of the availability of their songs for free on the web, I couldn't care less. However, I think what is more the case is that they are losing sales to the internet itself, as a result of the blossoming of grassroots musical culture that the internet is fostering.

"GIVING AWAY MUSIC HURTS SMALL ARTISTS"
This is an argument the RIAA is fond of putting forward. Sadly, many other independent recording artists believe it. They seem to think that if the major artists are losing sales to the internet, it must be happening to us, too. Either deliberately or through inaction, they don't put their music up on the web for free download. Fans of theirs, it often seems, respect this and don't put up the music, either (sometimes). I'm convinced this is all born out of confusion, and these artists are shooting themselves in the foot.

What's good for GM is definitely not what's good for the guy in Iowa City making electric cars in his garage. I constantly run into people who assume that I must be losing CD sales and suffering financially as a result of the fact that I put up all of my music on the web for free download. Sometimes they are artists who think I'm something of a scab. Other times they're fans who appreciate the free music and are concerned for my financial well-being.

Principles aside for the moment, on a purely practical level, the reality is that many independent artists, most definitely including myself, have benefited from the phenomenon of the free MP3. Like others, the fact that I'm making a living at all at music—unlike the overwhelming majority of musicians—is largely attributable to the internet, and specifically to free downloads.

It's not simple, and it's fairly easy to hypothesize one thing or another and back it up with selective information. But overall, my experience has been that I sold a few thousand CD's a year before the internet, and have continued to sell a few thousand CD's a year after the internet. Gig offers and fans in far-off places have multiplied, however, and in so many of these cases it's clear that they first heard my music on the internet, usually because someone they know guided them to my website.

Every year, over 100,000 songs are downloaded for free from my website, and many more from many other websites where they are hosted in one form or another. This represents many times what CD sales could possibly have been for me without a major record contract prior to the internet. My conclusion is that the free download phenomenon behaves more like radio airplay that I never would otherwise have had . And it's international airplay that has led to tours in countries around the world, and to gigs in remote corners of the US that are a direct result from someone telling someone else about songs of mine they found online for free.

The reality, pop stars aside, is that the overwhelming majority of musicians who are able to make a living from their music make it from performing. For DIY musicians who are not having their tours booked by Sony BMG's booking agencies, the most valuable resource are fans, especially the ones who are well-organized and enthusiastic enough that they want to organize a gig for us somewhere. Through fans like this, we can cobble together another tour. This process has been helped immensely by "viral marketing," the buzz that can happen when the music people like is freely available on the web.

I'm sure that there are many people who would have bought my latest CD if they weren't able to download it for free. Of this there is no doubt. But to think that this is therefore how the free download phenomenon works in general is extremely simplistic. For every person who downloads the songs instead of buying the CD, I'd guess there are 100 who hear the music on the web for the first time, who would probably never have heard it otherwise. For every 100 people who hear the music for free, say one of them will buy a CD to support the artist. For every 1,000, maybe one will organize a paying gig. This may not cause a big rise in CD sales, but ultimately it doesn't hurt them, either; and what it does for sure is dramatically increase the overall audience of independent artists around the world.

"BUT PEOPLE ARE STEALING PRIVATE PROPERTY ON THOSE P2P NETWORKS"

There are many ways to try to compensate artists for original work, scientists for ground-breaking research, inventors for great new inventions, etc. There is no single, sacred way to do this. There are many ways to support art and artists in society and reward them for their work. Paying royalties based on airplay, downloads and/or CD sales is one way among many.

If royalties are going to be a primary way artists are compensated, there are many ways to do this, too. With CD sales, according to the current system, the songwriter gets something like 7 cents per song per CD sold in the stores. With radio airplay, the onus on paying the royalties that may eventually get to some of the artists is on the radio stations; and the radio stations are usually supported by corporate advertisers.

If the RIAA really thought their artists could compete with the rest of the world's artists on a relatively open playing field, they'd probably be busily trying to create some kind of web-based infrastructure where corporate advertising would pay some kind of royalties for their artists. If this infrastructure existed, people would drift towards it as the path of least resistance, compared to finding music on P2P networks.

The problem is, the RIAA doesn't control the internet the way they control the commercial radio airwaves, and they know that the musical tastes of the people are broadening, and threatening their pop star system, threatening their profit margins. They can't keep out the competition, so they're trying hard to control the environment in a way that's most beneficial to their corporate interests—screw everybody else. Screw independent artists, and screw the public at large.

I don't know if anybody can predict with certainty, but it seems to me the basic nature of the internet will ultimately triumph over the narrow interests of the music industry. The music industry will not cease to exist by any means, but it will shrink somewhat, and will have to give way to the flourishing, grassroots music scene that the internet has nurtured.

It seems to me that the most relevant question in terms of the efforts of the RIAA is, at what cost to society at large? How far will they go to maintain this broken system, to maintain the inequities of their star-making machinery?

And another crucial question: why should a system be allowed to continue that massively rewards a few artists for their "original" records full of "original" songs, while leaving destitute the masses of musicians and others who created the cultural seas in which these "original" artists swim?

Musicians, as a whole, represent some of the richest people in the society—and many of the poorest. The music industry's system, in conceptual terms and in practical terms, is broken. It represents the interests of the monopolies against the interests of the rest of the world's people, cultures, musical traditions and musical innovations.

To my fellow musicians I say put all your music up for free download, help your careers and screw the music industry. To music fans I say keep on downloading, don't feel bad about it—and try not to get caught.

BIOGRAPHY

David Rovics has been called the musical voice of the progressive movement in the US. Amy Goodman has called him "the musical version of Democracy Now!" Since the mid-90's, Rovics has spent most of his time on the road, playing hundreds of shows every year throughout North America, Europe, Latin America, the Middle East and Japan. He and his songs have been featured on national radio programs in the US, Canada, Britain, Ireland, Italy, Sweden, Denmark and elsewhere. He has shared the stage regularly with leading intellectuals (Noam Chomsky, Howard Zinn), activists (Medea Benjamin, Ralph Nader), politicians (Dennis Kucinich, George Galloway), musicians (Billy Bragg, the Indigo Girls), and celebrities (Martin Sheen, Susan Sarandon). He has performed at dozens of massive rallies throughout North America and Europe and at thousands of conferences, college campuses and folk clubs throughout the world. In recent years he's added children's music and essay-writing to his repertoire. More importantly, he's really good. He will make you laugh, he will make you cry, and he will make the revolution irresistible.

www.davidrovics.com (main website)
www.myspace.com/davidrovics
www.soundclick.com/davidrovics (free mp3's)
www.songwritersnotebook.blogspot.com (essays)

PM Press was founded in 2007 as an independent publisher with offices in the US and UK, and a veteran staff boasting a wealth of experience in print and online publishing. Operating our own printing press enables us to print and distribute short as well as large run projects, timely texts and out of print classics.

We seek to create radical and stimulating fiction and non-fiction books, pamphlets, t-shirts, visual and audio materials to entertain, educate and inspire you. We aim to distribute these through every available channel with every available technology. Whether that means you are seeing anarchist classics at our bookfair stalls, reading our latest vegan cookbook at the café over (your third) microbrew, downloading geeky fiction e-books, or digging new music and timely videos from our website.

PM Press is always on the lookout for talented and skilled volunteers, artists, activists and writers to work with. If you have a great idea for a project or can contribute in some way, please get in touch.

PM Press . PO Box 23912 . Oakland CA 94623

www.pmpress.org